Silent Chaos

MARISSA KINGSLEY

Copyright © 2023 Marissa Kingsley

All rights reserved. No part of this book may be reproduced in any form without permission from the author, except as permitted by U.S. copyright law.

TABLE OF CONTENTS

SILENT CHAOS	1
STRUGGLE	2
WORRY	13
MOURN	24
LOSE CONTROL	33
HIDE	40
QUESTION	49
CHANGE	58
CHALLENGE	65
LET GO	72
OVERCOME	79
ENCOURAGE	88
LOVE	97

SILENT CHAOS

It's too quiet.
Too easy to think.
Images play like a projection.
Emotions heightened and alert,
With no switch to power down.
The desires, the dreams,
The uncertainties, the doubt,
The past, the future, and the now.
A break from interaction,
But even in silence,
There is chaos.

STRUGGLE

Today's struggle is tomorrow's progress, next month's growth, and lasting strength.

360

From every sunrise to every sunset,
From every good morning,
To every goodnight.
Everything that's in between
Mirrors the previous rotation.
Every day, trapped in a loop of mediocrity.
But nothing is done.
Nothing is changed.
We just keep spinning.

POWER OUTAGE

Candles flicker, lights go dim,
The glow perishes from deep within.
Frozen in the dark, trying to move around,
Paralyzed by fear and the absence of sound.
Unsure and lost, looking to get on track,
Desperately needing to escape from the black.
Scared and alone, searching for the light,
Anxious to emerge and have the courage to fight.

UNSPOKEN

Short for words,
Disappointed again,
Longing to say what was left unsaid.

Grasping the moment,
Attempting to be in control,
Why I can't speak to you,
I really don't know.

Nervous and timid,
Apprehensive and shy,
My words are contained,
They're locked inside.

Captive like a prisoner,
Hidden deep within,
Trying to break out,
And find a way to begin.

Tongue-tied and uneasy,
Cautious and safe,
The words exit my mind,
My thoughts are erased.

With a need to escape,
Yet an urge to hide,
My feelings are real,
But my words I can't find.

Not knowing the truth,
My heart left broken,
I barricade my words,
Those left unspoken.

PUZZLE PIECES

I wish I could string the right words together
That would mimic how I feel.

I wish I could convey those deep sentiments
That would illustrate what is real.

The confines of language
They limit and they trap,
Forcing us to settle,
Struggle and adapt.

PRISONER

The walls are getting closer—tighter.
She is struggling to breathe.
The still images are moving—talking.
Somehow, they all know her name.
The innocent children are evil—menacing.
Her paranoia is increasing.
Thoughts are taking her hostage—capturing.
Her freedom permitted no more.

WHITE NOISE

Clear voices jumbled,
Fading and incoherent.
The sound of silence,
Desirable and appealing.
Longing for coherence and relief,
I want to make it stop.
I need to make it stop.
How do I make it stop?

ROUGH ~~DRAFT~~ DROUGHT

It sits…
Bare and devoid.
Deprived of perspective and craving meaning.
The empty lines,
Flowing continuously without interruption.
No imprint nor reflection,
No sentiment nor rhyme,
The words escape and vacate,
They are not enough.

STORM

The darkness follows,
An encompassing shadow.
I move, it moves.
It dissipates, but restores.
I cower, I break, I fall like the rain,
But it is I, that is the creator.

VILLAIN

Sabotage the path,
Undermine the progress,
Overwhelm with doubt.
I am the antagonist of my story.

WORRY

No amount of worrying can alter the future, but we can't stop ourselves from doing it anyway.

PANIC

The feeling is growing,
Thoughts I can't divert,
I'm falling,
I'm lost,
I'm going to get hurt.
I analyze, I make lists,
Trying to prepare,
Run every scenario,
So I am aware.
Every day is different,
And it is tough to predict,
I can look for a distraction,
But my mind can't resist.
I can tell anyone
The best advice,
But when it comes to myself,
It's never alright.
Sometimes it's at night,
The ominous shadows in my dreams,
Sometimes it's too much,
Forced to hold back a scream.
It can be in the morning,
A struggle to get out of bed,
The fast, heavy breaths,
Images filling me with dread.
Sometimes it's all day,
And nobody knows but me,

It's not something that is pretty,
That anyone wants to see.
You can't explain it,
And it's hard to understand.
It's so easily dismissed,
And then it gets out of hand.
So I often keep it hidden,
Afraid that they won't care,
I try to calm down with logic,
But I'm still scared.

SIGNIFICANTLY INSIGNIFICANT

This might not matter anymore in
...days.
...months.
...years.
Or even in an hour.
It will disappear from consciousness,
Feeling as insignificant as the last forgotten fear.
But in that moment, it is everything.

ANXIETY SCROLL

Clicks on a keyboard,
Taps on a phone,
Looking for answers
On all the pages shown.

Contradicting information,
So many conflicting views,
Confusing partial "answers,"
All my findings skewed.

But I need an absolute conclusion,
A way for my nerves to settle down,
So I search for that definitive resolution,
…Page 404 not found.

THE WEIGHT OF WHAT IF'S

Asking the same questions,
To get the same answers,
Fishing for what I want to hear.

Coming up with the same logic,
To come to the same results,
But somehow it's anything but clear.

Playing it all over,
Just to replay it again,
Please tell me that comfort is near.

AFRAID TO BE HAPPY

Everything is great,
But nothing is okay,
Something will go wrong,
Because life finds a way.

I can't accept the calm,
So the clouds will roll in,
The sun cannot come out,
Even if the storm's within.

And all those words you say,
I want to believe, I do,
But I will question their validity,
Even if they're all true.

Maybe it's my anxiety
Or cynicism to accuse,
But it's hard not to be afraid,
When you have so much to lose.

CATASTROPHIZE

Dwell on what happened,
Plan for what's next,
Fear the unexpected.
Never in the moment.
Never enjoying the times we had
Once looked forward to.

INSOMNIA

I stare at the ceiling
As I lie awake in bed,
Counting the hours I might sleep
If I could just get out of my head.

ASTRAY

A series of obstacles
I render impassable.
No illuminated trail,
Nor visible signs.
Terrified the journey won't lead to the desired end
And I will be incomplete.

PREDICTED PROBLEMS

Will it, won't it?
You can't be sure,
Strategize regardless,
Longing to feel secure.

But nothing can be solved
Before it transpires,
No facts for solution,
No grounds for cease fire.

Halt the crisis,
Perhaps learn a thing or two,
Postpone those troubles,
Trust in future you.

MOURN

If it was a long time, if it was a short time. I was lucky to know you. Drifted, gone, or lost. I can visit you in the memories we created.

STATIC

Even if someone leaves,
The pictures still remain.
These moments live in a time
When our reality was different.
Those memories won't disappear,
No matter how hard you try.
But maybe,
That isn't always a bad thing.

MISSED

We hoped before we knew,
We dreamt before we saw,
We loved before we lost.

THE GUEST LIST

I couldn't anticipate,
I wasn't prepared,
A presence taken for granted,
And now you're not there.

In my memory you'll stay,
Because you shouldn't be so easy to erase,
But sometimes you're just gone,
With a simple backspace.

BOY FRIEND

Elementary school friends,
Picked on and teased,
Just childhood innocence,
Brought to its knees.

We were just kids
Who couldn't ignore what was said,
Endured it for years,
But it failed in the end.

I think about it often,
How you didn't think about it before,
You joked and you pushed
Till we weren't friends anymore.

MOSAIC

Through our lives,
We are influenced by so many people.
The distinctive phrases they say,
Their mannerisms,
What they teach us,
Their favorite things.
It all becomes a part of us.
It is these characteristics that make it much more difficult.
If they leave, just these pieces of them are left behind.
But it is also a way we can remember and keep them with us.

CASUALTY

Their overwhelming joy,
A gift not just for me.
The devastation of the letdown,
I could not prepare.

DEFEAT

I need to be in control,
But it's out of my hands,
I need to make this better,
But I can't make demands.
It's hard to keep it together when you're back at start,
Watching all that you've wanted fall apart.

THE DAY THAT WASN'T

We waited,
We dreamt,
We planned.
Everything was ready,
Everything was perfect,
Everything was right.
Until it wasn't.

LOSE CONTROL

You can grasp to hang on. You can fight to remain in charge. But it is easy to let it slip away.

LIMBO

How can I escape the in between?
An undetermined route
Creating an unnerving question mark.
An incomplete chapter that will write itself,
The answers hanging in the balance,
Waiting to fill the page.

BURST

When guarded optimism
Turns to defensive pessimism,
The "when" becomes "if."

BLACK SWAN

The changes are subtle,
The glow steadily dimming,
Emerging from sheltered existence.

The transformation is drastic,
But you don't realize it's happening,
Until the light goes dark.

COLLAPSE

I know it's irrational,
I hear myself spiral,
Feel the drift from reason,
When I know control is vital.

I see myself falter
And I see myself fall,
It's either everything's together,
Or nothing at all.

But I know my way,
I see with perfect clarity,
Still I watch my demise,
From a place of sanity.

EXPECTATIONS

Playing it over,
How it should go,
Learned and rehearsed,
Guaranteed to flow.

My planned conversations,
The important parts you skip,
Why aren't you following along,
Cause now we've gone off script.

This wasn't my objective,
Were you distracted or misled?
Why couldn't you recite
What I had in my head.

WHAT SOBER DOESN'T SAY

I should have known better,
This I will regret,
I may not remember,
But you will not forget.

Glasses empty,
Room is spinning,
It's all fun and games,
But I'm not winning.

Not in control,
They'll be no guessing,
My brain says no,
But my mouth is confessing.

Trying to be coy,
But there is only trouble,
Taking advantage of my mind
While I'm seeing double.

HIDE

Concealing your beliefs, your feelings, your emotions. You may believe it is the only way until you can find yourself.

MESSAGES I'LL NEVER SEND

Hello,
How have you been?
I really miss you,
Do you remember the times when…?

Dear friend,
Why did you leave?
Did I do something wrong?
Did it have to do with me?

Sorry to bother you,
I just want you to know,
You've truly changed my life,
Please don't ever go.

I know it's been a while,
I don't know what it was about,
Can we put it behind us?
Can we try and work it out?

I know I said I forgave you,
I did say it was okay,
But I don't think you realize,
It hurts me every day.

I type it out,
Read it to the end,
Close out the entry,
Never pressing send.

UNPUBLISHED

Years of words
Hesitant to share,
But my diary only half revealed.
Lines still imprisoned under lock and key,
Too vulnerable to exist.
Infinite ideas yearning to become something beautiful
Remain crossed out and abandoned.

FILTER ME

Adjust the levels,
Blur the lines,
Perfect the imperfect.
An artificial reflection of the truth
That creates a flawless illusion
And conceals the beauty of time.

DETACHED

Don't show interest,
Pretend not to care,
Avoid eye contact,
Imagine they're not there.

Distance yourself,
Don't get attached,
Once you do,
There's no going back.

The feelings you have,
You must deceive,
If you don't let them in,
They can't leave.

TABOO

Trapped in corners,
Absent in speech,
Those suppressed emotions,
Suspended from reach.

Discouraged to speak aloud,
Dismissed if we did,
Avoid the uncomfortable,
They're better off hid.

Forced to suffer in silence,
Because we mustn't recount,
Those truths barred and restricted,
Those realities we're not supposed to talk about.

COME OUT, COME OUT, WHEREVER YOU ARE

I hide, you seek.
You hide, I seek.
Count to ten.
Hide in small, dark spaces
Knowing eventually, you will be found.
Over and over…
Until you get too good at hiding.
Until no one even knows they are supposed to seek.
Until it is no longer a game.
I want to be found,
But nobody is looking.
I don't want to play anymore.

CLIFF NOTES

Half honest with fake smiles
And a counterfeit disposition.
The narrative I chose to show.
A shield from the questions,
The prying,
The curious,
Lying for preservation.
But at what point am I lying to myself?

UNIFORM

Overlooked if simple,
Avoided if original,
Censored and reduced,
Compelled to stand in the middle.
Easily reproduced, duplicated, or traced,
Pressured to be a copy and paste.

QUESTION

I wonder if you met someone when you were both at another point in your lives than when you did, if things would have been different.

BUTTERFLY EFFECT

Do you ever wonder how many lives you have affected,
For better or for worse?
Or how many people's memories you are in
Even if you don't remember them?
Every day, every minute, every second of our lives
We are in someone else's, whether we know it or not.
Every encounter can stay with someone forever.
Every action, however inconsequential we assume it is,
Can make the first domino topple.
We are often oblivious to it.
But if we did know,
Would it make a difference?

PERCEPTION

I'm always the same,
But to each person I am different.

I can modify my role and adjust my approach,
But to me, I'm still the same.

For sure I'll never know,
But it scares me to think,
That the way I see myself,
Is not the way they see me.

GORGEOUS

Out of your grasp,
Distant but there,
A smile, a hello,
A deep longing stare.

Unfamiliar nerves,
Confidence that breaks,
A new hesitation,
A steady voice now shakes.

Your undivided attention,
Desire driving you mad,
Is it what you want?
Or do we want what we can't have?

GEMINI

What would you think
If you saw the other side?
All of what I'm ashamed of,
Those secrets I try to hide.

I'm jealous,
I'm selfish,
And patience I lack,
I'm petty,
I'm anxious, I easily crack.

I'll be passive aggressive,
I'll manipulate,
I'll coerce,
You like me at my best,
But would you love me at my worst?

NEW YEARS DAY

Make them,
Break them,
Forget them.
The same words we say year after year.
Optimistic goals lacking effort.
Will this time be different?
Will you be different?

SACRIFICE

Think about everything you have
And everything you've lost.
Was the loss a consequence
Or a casualty of the gain?
Did you lose someone?
Did you lose yourself?
Was it worth it?

HE SAID, SHE SAID

You speak, I listen,
But is it true?
You can only surmise
With a limited view.

Detailed yet concise,
Still impossible to decide,
Cause it's easy to believe a lie,
When you only know one side.

DREAMS

Familiar faces from a lifetime ago,
Randomly placed without prior thought.
Why the recollection?
Meaningful or insignificant?
Do I ever appear to them?

CHANGE

Pages finish, chapters end, books close…but you can start a new story.

THE CONSTANT

People and places that used to be constant,
Become non-existent in our reality.
Feelings and habits that were comfortable,
Become lost in the past.
Faint recollections, unaffected by their absence,
Or painful losses and reoccurring heartbreak.
Some inevitable,
Some unwelcome,
But we're forced to adjust to new constants,
Until they change again.

FLY

Packed up boxes,
Old pictures in frames,
Of friends and of moments
You hoped never would change.

History beneath the dust,
The past frozen in time,
Stories long completed,
Feelings expressed in a rhyme.

Nostalgic to reminisce,
But faced with mourning what has passed,
Those times we took for granted,
Those times that went too fast.

NOSTALGIA

It was just a building,
But the memories it housed,
Wouldn't have existed without.

It was just some friends,
Some lost, some remain,
Their presence I would never change.

It was just a small part of our lives,
We couldn't have stayed,
Unexpected, the impact it made.

UNFRIENDED

Reasons unspoken,
Too much time,
Too much space?
Dissimilar journeys?
Or easy to replace?

Uncertain the cause,
Debatable what's to blame,
Because nothing happened,
But everything changed.

GENERIC SENTIMENTS

Take no time,
Write with no thought,
Simple and plain,
As the card that was bought.

Standard greeting,
Complimentary close,
Expressing no care,
My disconnect shows.

FLASH

60…59…58…57…56…55…54…53…52…51…50
It seems like an insubstantial amount of time,
49…48…47…46…45…44…43…42…41…40
But all it takes is a blink,
39…38…37…36…35…34…33…32…31…30
Events, actions, or consequences,
29…28…27…26…25…24…23…22…21…20
Whether unintentional or linked.
19…18…17…16…15…14…13…12…11…10
An instance of clarity, tragedy, bravery, or ignorance,
9…8…7…6…5…4…3…2…1
One minute can make all the difference.

CHALLENGE

Challenge your limits. Challenge others. Maybe you will learn something about yourself. Maybe you will learn something about them.

INSPIRE ME

Tell me
How you see the world,
Show me
How you've grown to feel.
Allow me
To know the darkest parts.
Help me
Understand what is real.

DANGEROUS GAME

Move your piece,
And I'll move mine,
Let's play a game,
Ready your line.

Black and white,
Diagonal and across,
Make decisions wisely,
Or all will be lost.

Position your knight,
And move your rook,
Proceed with strength,
Or fight for what was took.

Challenge with caution,
Cause rest assured,
Blink too much,
And I'll take yours.

DARE ME

Words are powerful,
Don't pretend—you knew,
But you can't tell me what I can't do.

I can't help it,
You're in my head,
I'll hold on to what you said.

Make no mistake,
It won't last long,
Because I will use it
To prove you wrong.

SOCIETY SAYS

Invented standards.
Inane guidelines.
Not detrimental to stray,
Nor essential to adhere.
Wholly nonsensical and trivial.
Who made these rules?
And why do you care if I break them?

INCONCEIVABLE

Faced with a situation,
Not possible to predict,
The changing variables too great to compare.

Running through the scenarios,
A positive outcome not guaranteed,
Questioning if I'm strong enough.

Searching for courage to proceed,
Still struggling to accept that I've found myself on a path
That I never imagined I'd walk.

INTERNAL CONFLICT

Opportunity versus time,
Hope versus defeat,
With the future on the line,
The urgency's increased.

But shot after shot,
With no sign of relief,
All the protections deteriorating,
Convinced the only outcome is grief.

Tempting to wave and surrender,
Signaling the suffering to cease,
Treat the broken and wounded,
Find some semblance of peace.

But what's easy to do isn't always easy to accept,
And the fears are all one sided,
Little faith of pulling through,
With reasoning divided.

Perhaps more regrettable to retreat,
Maybe a relentless advance is capable to compete.

And maybe it's not about keeping score,
When you're battling for something worth the war.

__LET GO__

Sometimes, you just need to let go and see what happens.

LIBERATION

Release the notions, the words, and the pain that is holding you back.
Your past is not your future.

UNLOAD

The unpredictable outcomes,
The daunting anticipation,
The heavy weight of the unknown.
It is too much to carry.
It is too much wasted time.
Unburden from the circumstances that are uncontrollable.
Refocus on what is.

THE UNEXPECTED

5 years ago…
Did you correctly imagine your life as it is today?
1 year ago…
Did you expect all that has happened since then?
3 months ago…
Was everything exactly the same as it is now?
Hope, plan, imagine.
But oftentimes, life decides for itself.

TUNNEL VISION

Distracted focus,
A distorted view,
Rational thought compromised,
Objections misconstrued.

Overlooked opportunity,
With nothing special created,
An unhealthy fixation,
Leaving precious moments wasted.

Recognize the obsession,
Relinquish your internal war,
That keeps on convincing you
That you always need more.

TEMPORARY FIX

A stand in for the absent,
Your interest is fleeting,
A doll you'll replace,
And I'm not competing.

You may not realize,
And I was too blind to see,
That what you really need,
Does not equate to me.

A "love,"
A friend,
A comfort,
Take your pick,
What it comes down to,
Is a temporary fix.

JUST DANCE

Curtains opened or closed.
Eyes watching or not.
Free the bottled-up stress and anxiety,
Anger and sadness,
Happiness and doubt.
Whatever the emotion,
Dance it out.

OVERCOME

Never let fear hold you back. Take your time, be afraid, but do it anyway.

RISE

Hesitant to act,
Stomach in knots,
Intense, the anxiety it brings.
But sometimes, there are more important things.

SOUND OFF

Calculated approach,
You take advantage of the silence.
An agreeable target
That's too scared to move.
But now it's time to fight back.

BULLY

It is okay if it doesn't scare you,
It scares me.
It is okay if you don't understand it,
It is clear to me.
It is okay if it isn't your passion,
It is mine.
Your words carry no weight.

ENEMY

The reasons are excuses,
The limitations are assumed,
The fear is temporary.
The only hindrance is yourself.

MIND GAMES

Innumerable hurdles,
A certain defeat,
A captive critic of my mind.

But this is a challenge
That I can beat,
And make it to the finish line.

PEER PRESSURE

Can and can't.
Should and shouldn't.

No means no,
And maybe doesn't mean yes.

Manipulated to feel like the choice was yours.
Intimidated to fall in line.

Resist uniformity,
Reject coercion,
Disconnect the noise,
Take the power.

MORAL COMPASS

Right or wrong,
Good or bad.
Angel on the right,
Devil on the left.
But it's not all black and white.
The middle can decide.

HERO

Discover the path,
Strengthen the progress,
Conquer the doubt.
I am the protagonist of my story.

ENCOURAGE

We only focus on how far we have left to go, and we forget to look back at how far we have already come.

SINFULLY UNAWARE

Blind to your passion,
Your creativity,
Your beauty.
Crippled by your anxiety,
Your fear,
Your past.
Despite the encouragement,
The words,
The actions,
It's never enough.
I wish you could see
Through my eyes
The way I see you.

STRUT

Walk with confidence,
Command the room,
Keep your head high,
Don't let the heels wear you.

REPLICA

A mirror cannot capture your energy,
Your kindness,
Your worth.

It does not capture how your eyes light up
When you're doing something you love,
Or all that you have accomplished.

A mirror is not a true reflection.
It does not tell a story.
It is not *you*.

THE SCENIC ROUTE

Constant fluctuation,
The road not paved,
An indirect course.
But regardless of the detour,
You will arrive at the correct destination.

DEAR PAST SELF

You feel like you hit a wall.
That you're not capable or deserving.
You feel restricted by your apprehension.
You can overcome this.
You do overcome this.
You won't believe all that you will do.

DEAR FUTURE SELF

I hope you are at a place where you accomplished and gained all that you were fighting for.
Maybe now you're striving for new dreams,
Or you are struggling with new troubles.
Remember, that you have been here before and you prevailed.
Keep pushing and growing.
Keep creating and dreaming.
You got this.
You always have.

MINDFULNESS

When I can't process all that is on my mind,
I remember you reminding me, "one day at a time."

OPTIMIST

Someday, you'll have your "someday."
The impossible will be possible.
Problems will become opportunities.
Dreams will overshadow nightmares.
Your story will help others navigate theirs.

LOVE

Life can throw some curveballs, but even when it feels like it is all falling apart, you make sure we stay whole.

NOT ANOTHER CLICHÉ LOVE POEM

Beating heart,
Fluttering wings,
Silly love songs,
And birds that sing.

Broken speech,
An inadvertent twirl,
Writing your last name as mine,
Like an obsessed schoolgirl.

But I'll keep my distance,
I'll take my time,
And wait for the moment,
Your eyes meet mine.

EARENDEL

Love is often measured with figurative language,
Each one trying to raise the bar,

They say:
"I love you to the moon and back,"
But the moon isn't really that far.

So instead, I'm going to tell you:
"I love you to the furthest discovered star."

SISTER

Similar look,
Similar interests,
Similar way we think,
Always competitive by nature,
& constantly in sync.

We have fought,
We have learned,
We have grown,
My first best friend
That I met at home.

We made a bond you can't match,
& an unbreakable guarantee,
That I'll always have you,
& you'll always have me.

A – TEAM

The sudden turbulence
That's scary and intense,
It's fleeting but merciless,
And I need to find my way home.

…So I make the call.

Better than an antidote,
A vital lifeline
Keeping me afloat,
I am not alone.

NO DOUBT

I doubt many things,
But I never doubted the way I feel about you.
I question my decisions,
But I have never questioned us.
I pictured how life could have played out differently,
But I never pictured living without you.

THE END

I love…
My intellect,
My imagination,
My drive.

I love…
My flaws,
My imperfections,
My weaknesses.

All of the complexities and traits,
All of them are me.

www.ingramcontent.com/pod-product-compliance
Lightning Source LLC
Chambersburg PA
CBHW050437010526
44118CB00013B/1571